<h1 style="text-align:center">はしがき</h1>

　本書『Active　Practical Reading 完成編』は，大学入学共通テスト，英検®，GTEC®に対応した速読問題集です。近年のリーディングの問題では，大意把握や情報検索といった速読の力がますます重要になってきています。そのため本書では，与えられた英文から必要な情報を短時間で見つけ出す「スキャニング（探し読み）」の技能を，"Practice makes perfect!"（習うより慣れよ。）を実践しながら身につけることができるように構成しました。各レッスンで用意した実用的で多様な英文と設問を通して，本書がみなさんの大学入試に向けた英語学習に役立つことを期待しています。

【本書の構成と利用法】

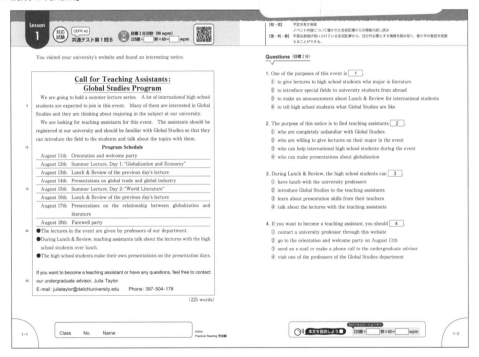

●本文

・各試験の英文形式に対応した本文です。

・本書ではレッスンが進むにつれて，1分あたりに読むべき語数（wpm）がだんだん多くなるように目標時間を設定しています。上部（🕑）の計算式を使って，読みの速度を算出してみましょう。

・二次元コードを読み取って，本文の音声をPCやスマートフォンから聞くことができます。（英文形式によって，一部の音声が収録されていないレッスンがあります。）

●設問

・各試験の設問形式に対応した設問です。（設問数は異なります。）

・求められる「知識・技能」と「思考力・判断力・表現力」をページ上部（【知・技】【思・判・表】）に示しました。

・スピーキング・トレーナーを使って，本文の音読練習をすることができます。下部の計算式を使って，1分あたりに音読できた語数（wpm）を算出してみましょう。

CONTENTS

Lesson	対応試験		テキストタイプ	本文語数	目標 wpm	
1	共通テスト	第1問B	告知記事	225 words	90 wpm	
2	英検®準2級	第4部A	メール	246 words	90 wpm	
3	共通テスト	第1問B	ポスター	267 words	90 wpm	
4	共通テスト	第2問B	ネット記事	253 words	90 wpm	
5	GTEC® 英検®準2級	パートC 第4部B	説明文	250 words	90 wpm	
6	共通テスト	第2問B	記事+メール	301 words	95 wpm	
7	英検®準2級	第4部A	メール	281 words	95 wpm	
8	共通テスト	第3問B	雑誌記事	302 words	95 wpm	
9	GTEC® 英検®準2級	パートC 第4部B	説明文	320 words	95 wpm	
10	共通テスト	第3問B	雑誌記事	316 words	95 wpm	
11	GTEC® 英検®2級	パートC 第3部BC	説明文	354 words	100 wpm	
12	共通テスト	第4問	記事+グラフ	409 words	100 wpm	
13	共通テスト	第5問	物語文	425 words	100 wpm	
14	共通テスト	第6問A	記事	421 words	100 wpm	
15	共通テスト	第6問B	新聞記事	373 words	100 wpm	
16	GTEC® 英検®2級	パートC 第3部BC	説明文	421 words	100 wpm	
17	共通テスト	第4問	レポート+グラフ	523 words	110 wpm	
18	共通テスト	第5問	雑誌記事	496 words	110 wpm	
19	共通テスト	第6問A	記事	524 words	110 wpm	
20	共通テスト	第6問B	記事	492 words	110 wpm	

求められる資質・能力	
知識・技能	思考力・判断力・表現力
□予定を表す表現／□イベント内容について書かれた告知記事からの情報の探し読み	□平易な表現が用いられている告知記事から，自分が必要とする情報を読み取り，書き手の意図を把握することができる。
□環境・リサイクルに関する表現／□イベントについて書かれたメールからの情報の探し読み	□身近な話題に関して平易な英語で書かれた短いメールを読んで，概要を把握することができる。
□イベント内容について書かれたポスターからの情報の探し読み	□平易な表現が用いられているポスターから，自分が必要とする情報を読み取り，書き手の意図を把握することができる。
□情報機器に関する表現／□ネット記事からの情報機器についての情報や，その意見内容に関する情報の探し読み	□身近な話題に関して平易な英語で書かれた短い説明を読んで，概要や要点をとらえたり，情報を事実と意見に整理することができる。
□生き物の生態に関する表現／□ウミガメについて書かれた説明文からの情報の探し読み	□身近な話題に関して平易な英語で書かれた短い説明を読んで，概要を把握することができる。
□環境に関する表現／□海洋プラスチック汚染について書かれた記事とメールからの情報の探し読み	□身近な話題に関して平易な英語で書かれた短い説明を読んで，概要や要点をとらえたり，推測したり，情報を事実と意見に整理することができる。
□誘う［提案する］表現／□旅行日程について書かれたメールからの情報の探し読み	□身近な話題に関して平易な英語で書かれた短いメールを読んで，概要を把握することができる。
□暦に関する表現／□文化について書かれた雑誌記事からの情報の探し読み	□平易な英語で書かれた短い説明を読んで，概要を把握することができる。
□AI・科学技術の発展と職業に関する表現／□AI・科学技術の発展と職業について書かれた説明文からの情報の探し読み	□平易な英語で書かれた短い説明を読んで，概要を把握することができる。
□結婚式について書かれた雑誌記事からの情報の探し読み	□平易な英語で書かれた短い物語を読んで，概要を把握することができる。
□国旗とその色について書かれた説明文からの情報の探し読み	□短い説明を読んで，概要を把握することができる。
□通貨や経済に関する表現／□経済について書かれた雑誌記事からの情報の探し読み	□比較的短い記事，資料などから，自分が必要とする情報を読み取り，論理の展開や書き手の意図を把握することができる。
□英語教育経験について書かれた物語文からの情報の探し読み	□短い物語を読んで，概要を把握することができる。
□IoT について書かれた記事からの情報の探し読み	□身近な話題に関する記事を読んで概要や要点を把握したり，情報を整理したりすることができる。また，文章の論理展開を把握したり，要約することができる。
□漫画に関する表現／□文化について書かれた新聞記事からの情報の探し読み	□なじみのある社会的な話題に関する記事を読んで概要や要点を把握したり，情報を整理したりすることができる。また，文章の論理展開を把握したり，要約することができる。
□食生活に関する表現／□ダイエット方法について書かれた説明文からの情報の探し読み	□短い説明を読んで，概要を把握することができる。
□自動運転について書かれたレポートからの情報の探し読み	□比較的短いレポート，資料などから，自分が必要とする情報を読み取り，論理の展開や書き手の意図を把握することができる。
□地域と産業について書かれた雑誌記事からの情報の探し読み	□短い記事を読んで，概要を把握することができる。
□音楽と医療に関する表現／□音楽療法について書かれた記事からの情報の探し読み	□なじみのある社会的な話題に関する記事を読んで概要や要点を把握したり，情報を整理したりすることができる。また，文章の論理展開を把握したり，要約することができる。
□食品廃棄について書かれた記事からの情報の探し読み	□なじみのある社会的な話題に関する記事を読んで概要や要点を把握したり，情報を整理したりすることができる。また，文章の論理展開を把握したり，要約することができる。

Lesson
1

対応試験

CEFR A2
共通テスト第1問B

目標2分30秒 (90 wpm)
225語÷□秒×60=□wpm

You visited your university's website and found an interesting notice.

Call for Teaching Assistants: Global Studies Program

We are going to hold a summer lecture series. A lot of international high school students are expected to join in this event. Many of them are interested in Global Studies and they are thinking about majoring in the subject at our university.

We are looking for teaching assistants for this event. The assistants should be registered at our university and should be familiar with Global Studies so that they can introduce the field to the students and talk about the topics with them.

Program Schedule

August 11th	Orientation and welcome party
August 12th	Summer Lecture, Day 1: "Globalization and Economy"
August 13th	Lunch & Review of the previous day's lecture
August 14th	Presentations on global trade and global industry
August 15th	Summer Lecture, Day 2: "World Literature"
August 16th	Lunch & Review of the previous day's lecture
August 17th	Presentations on the relationship between globalization and literature
August 18th	Farewell party

●The lectures in the event are given by professors of our department.

●During Lunch & Review, teaching assistants talk about the lectures with the high school students over lunch.

●The high school students make their own presentations on the presentation days.

If you want to become a teaching assistant or have any questions, feel free to contact our undergraduate advisor, Julia Taylor.

E-mail: juliataylor@daiichiuniversity.edu   Phone: 397-504-178

(225 words)

Class	No.	Name	

Active
Practical Reading 完成編

Questions （目標2分）

1. One of the purposes of this event is ☐ 1 ☐.

   ① to give lectures to high school students who major in literature

   ② to introduce special fields to university students from abroad

   ③ to make an announcement about Lunch & Review for international students

   ④ to tell high school students what Global Studies are like

2. The purpose of this notice is to find teaching assistants ☐ 2 ☐.

   ① who are completely unfamiliar with Global Studies

   ② who are willing to give lectures on their major in the event

   ③ who can help international high school students during the event

   ④ who can make presentations about globalization

3. During Lunch & Review, the high school students can ☐ 3 ☐.

   ① have lunch with the university professors

   ② introduce Global Studies to the teaching assistants

   ③ learn about presentation skills from their teachers

   ④ talk about the lectures with the teaching assistants

4. If you want to become a teaching assistant, you should ☐ 4 ☐.

   ① contact a university professor through this website

   ② go to the orientation and welcome party on August 11th

   ③ send an e-mail or make a phone call to the undergraduate advisor

   ④ visit one of the professors of the Global Studies department

Lesson
2

対応試験

CEFR A2
英検®準2級 第4部A

目標2分45秒 (90 wpm)
246語÷ □ 秒×60= □ wpm

From: Amelia Harris <a-harris@endless-summer.com>
To: Lucas Stark <lucas2020@ymail.com>
Date: August 21
Subject: Endless Summer Festival

5　Hi, Lucas,

This is Amelia from Endless Summer.　Thank you for your e-mail.　We are happy to hear that you are interested in our festival.　We are going to hold two events at the end of September.　The first one is for collecting old clothes for recycling and will be held from September 21 to 23.　The second one is for people who want to

10　buy the clothes at reasonable prices.　It will be held from September 25 to 30.　We call these events the Endless Summer Festival.　The fee for each event is $8 for adults, $4 for children 3 to 14, and free for children under 3.

We first started this festival in 2013.　Since then, it has been becoming more and more popular in the local community.　The main purpose is to reduce trash in

15　homes.　You may have some good clothes that you have not worn for a long time. Should they just be thrown away or should they be recycled?　In the first event of our festival, you can sell your old clothes.　If your clothes are too worn out or too old to sell, you can donate them as well.　We can make new clothes from them.

You can download an application form from our website.　Please print it out and

20　bring it to the festival.　Please make sure to sign it.

Sincerely,
Amelia Harris

(246 words)

Class　　No.　　Name

Questions （目標2分）

1. Why is Amelia writing to Lucas?　　[1]
   ① To answer his questions about how to collect old clothes.
   ② To check his schedule in September.
   ③ To invite him to an event held on September 24.
   ④ To tell him more about the Endless Summer Festival.

2. What does Amelia say about children aged 3 to 14?　　[2]
   ① Their event fee is higher than that for adults.
   ② They are not old enough to participate in the event.
   ③ They can join the festival at half of the adult price.
   ④ They do not have to pay any fee for the festival.

3. What is the main purpose of this festival?　　[3]
   ① To boost consumers' spending on clothes.
   ② To cut down on waste at home by recycling clothes.
   ③ To recycle clothes to make new products such as plastic bottles.
   ④ To reduce trash at home by throwing away home items.

4. If you want to join the festival, you should [4] .
   ① invite a lot of guests and make a speech about them
   ② make an appointment with Amelia
   ③ send your application by e-mail
   ④ take your application to the festival

Lesson

3

対応試験

CEFR A2
共通テスト第1問B

目標3分 (90 wpm)
267語÷ [　] 秒×60= [　] wpm

You are visiting the library in your university. You have found a poster about an interesting event.

Phoenix University Presents

THE LEONARD LIBRARY BOOK AWARD 2020

with Prof. Steven Knight

What is the Leonard Library Book Award?

The award officially started on November 22, 1996. This annual book award has celebrated a wide variety of books from fiction to non-fiction. Every year, we offer a special section in the library for these books so that you can easily find them in our library. In addition, a professor at Phoenix University introduces the top three books of the year. This event is organized by Phoenix University.

Announcement of Special Interviews

This event is celebrating its 25th anniversary this year. We will invite the authors of the top three books to our event on this special occasion. You can listen to special talks by the authors themselves!

Date: From 4 p.m. to 6 p.m. on Monday, September 21

Place: Leonard Library Room 504

Titles	Authors	Comments from the authors
My New Love	Isabella Friedman	Why do we fall in love? In my lecture, we will explore human love from a philosophical point of view.
How to Be a Minimalist	David Bloomfield	Too much stuff in your house? I will tell you about three simple steps which will help you to throw things away.
On Reading	Andrew Willy	When you are reading a book, you are telling yourself a story. If you are objective, you will reach a new horizon of understanding. I'll explain this and more at my talk.

Prof. Steven Knight will conduct interviews with these three authors. You can ask them questions during the interviews, but the questions should be related to their books.

(267 words)

Class　　No.　　Name

Active
Practical Reading 完成編

Questions （目標2分）

1. The Leonard Library Book Award event is ☐ 1 ☐.
   ① introduced by university students
   ② organized by the authors of the top three books
   ③ presented by Phoenix University
   ④ presented to benefit university professors

2. This 2020 event is special because ☐ 2 ☐.
   ① a party to celebrate its 25th anniversary will be held
   ② the authors of the top three books are invited to the event
   ③ the library offers a special section for award-winning books
   ④ you can read articles about three authors there

3. You can learn about ☐ 3 ☐ from the three talks.
   ① how to communicate with other people
   ② interesting topics related to our lives
   ③ popular fantasy stories in novels
   ④ simple ideas about how to become a minimalist

4. At the event, you ☐ 4 ☐.
   ① can ask questions about the books
   ② must buy the three authors' books
   ③ should be ready to answer questions
   ④ will interview the three authors

Lesson
4

対応試験

CEFR A2

共通テスト第2問B

目標2分50秒（90 wpm）
253語÷ ☐ 秒×60= ☐ wpm

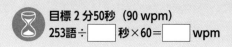

Your English teacher gave you an article to help you prepare for the debate in the next class.　Part of this article with one of the comments is shown below.

No Tablets in Schools!

By Sophia Smith, London

19 DECEMBER 2020, 4:07 PM

Today, it is difficult to imagine a life without digital devices such as smartphones. Even students at elementary schools have access to such digital devices.　Some schools in Japan are considering introducing tablet computers into their classes in order to replace textbooks.　However, there are a few things to be concerned about.

1. This will cost a lot of money.

A considerable amount of money is needed when tablets are introduced in a school.　If each student is given a tablet, the school needs a high-speed Internet connection to allow students to use their tablets.　Also, teachers need to attend training programs to learn how to use the tablets and software packages.　If schools must cover these expenses, the budget needed will be huge.

2. Reading is slower with digital text.

Studies have shown that students tend to read digital textbooks between 20 and 30 percent more slowly than printed textbooks.　This means that most students should read printed textbooks to understand and retain the information in them more efficiently.

3. Tablets may distract students from studying.

Some students become addicted to using their apps, emails and games.　They are easily tempted to use their tablet in class or at home for personal enjoyment.

---

38 Comments

Daniel Hornstein　19 December 2020, 6:11 PM

Digital textbooks have many advantages that printed textbooks do not have. Sticking to old-fashioned education styles is not enough to solve the problems schools are facing today.

(253 words)

Class　　No.　　Name

Active
Practical Reading 完成編

Questions（目標2分）

1. According to the passage, some schools in Japan are considering   1 .
   ① allowing their students to use their own mobile phones at school
   ② introducing tablet computers into their school curriculum for free
   ③ supplying tablet computers for the students to use in classes
   ④ teaching the teachers how to use tablet computers for their classes

2. Sophia thinks the introduction of tablet computers in schools   2 .
   ① can be helpful for students to learn subjects efficiently
   ② cause some problems for both schools and students
   ③ is due to our social dependence on digital devices
   ④ will not work well unless the government pays for it

3. One **fact** stated in Sophia's article is that   3 .
   ① schools have to pay the money related to introducing tablet computers
   ② students may use their tablets for different purposes than studying
   ③ students tend to read digital textbooks more slowly than printed textbooks
   ④ teachers are too busy to attend training programs to learn about digital devices

4. Which of the following pieces of information is helpful to make Daniel's opinion more persuasive?   4
   ① Digital textbooks can play audios and videos to help students understand what they are learning.
   ② Security management is important when using digital textbooks since students' learning histories are accumulated in their devices.
   ③ Students can write notes in their digital textbooks.
   ④ Using tablet computers for too long is highly likely to damage students' eyes.

Lesson 5

 対応試験 GTEC® パートC
英検®準2級 第4部B

CEFR A2

目標 2分45秒 (90 wpm)
250語÷ [ ] 秒×60= [ ] wpm

There are seven species of sea turtles worldwide. All of them are classified as endangered species. Unfortunately, humans are one of the reasons why these wonderful marine travelers are in danger of extinction.

Do you know how far sea turtles travel? Some species of sea turtles swim thousands
5 of miles throughout their lifetime to lay eggs on the same tiny island where their mothers laid their eggs.

About two decades ago, this was revealed by Adelita, a loggerhead sea turtle, which was caught by a fisherman in the Gulf of California. When she was captured, she was just the size of a big plate. Based on her size, she was just a few years old. Wallace J.
10 Nichols, a marine researcher, hit upon the idea of tracking Adelita across an entire ocean by using satellite tracking technology.

Adelita was released into the wild on August 10, 1996. Though she had been in captivity, she knew where she should go. At that time, the Internet was new to many people, but millions of kids shared her travel around the ocean on the Internet. Her
15 migration showed us that loggerheads born in Japan cross the Pacific and feed in California and Mexico before going back home to nest in Japan.

Today, we are driving sea turtles to extinction by our destruction of their nests and habitats, but this research on Adelita reminds us that the oceans are connected and that we need to work together to protect sea turtles and their habitats.

(250 words)

Class   No.   Name

Questions（目標2分）

1. What is this passage mainly about? 　1

① The destruction of sea turtles' habitats.

② The extinction of creatures in the sea.

③ The history of the migration of sea turtles.

④ The remarkable journeys of sea turtles.

2. According to the passage, what is one unique feature of sea turtles? 　2

① They lay eggs at the same place where their mothers laid their eggs.

② They have lived in harmony with human beings for a long time.

③ They share feeding and nesting areas together with other turtles.

④ They were once thought to be extinct.

3. What was revealed by tracking Adelita? 　3

① A long history of sea turtles.

② A mystery of sea turtles' migration.

③ A study about sea turtles in Japan.

④ A tendency of young Internet users.

4. What did we learn from Adelita? 　4

① The connection between satellite technology and information technology.

② The connections between human beings and sea turtles and their importance.

③ The connections of the oceans and the importance of protecting sea turtles and the oceans.

④ The unique aspects of sea turtles and the lifestyles of the people around them.

Lesson
6

対応試験
CEFR A2
共通テスト第2問B

目標 3 分10秒 （95 wpm）
301語÷ ☐ 秒×60= ☐ wpm

Takuro has written an article about plastic pollution in the ocean at university in England, where he is now studying as an exchange student. He has received a reply about the article from his professor.

Let's Discuss How to Reduce Plastic Wastes

Plastic pollution in the ocean is becoming a big problem around the world. When I saw pictures of beaches covered with pieces of plastic waste, I thought we had to change the current situation where single-use plastics are consumed in large quantities. A huge amount of plastic waste is thrown away into the ocean every year.

In order to remedy this situation, some restaurant chains in Japan have stopped using plastic straws and started using paper straws. "A lot of customers understand that they should not use plastic straws after learning that the change was for environmental reasons," said a restaurant manager. People may understand that environmental protection is more important than convenience.

The main purpose of this action is to show consumers how important it is to reduce plastic waste. It would be difficult to live without plastic products. However, now is the time when we should deal with the issues we are facing and change our lifestyles.

Re: Let's Discuss How to Reduce Plastic Wastes <Posted on 21 September 2022>
To: Takuro Matsuda
From: David Adger

Dear Takuro,

Thank you for sharing the information about Japan with our class. It may be a good idea to compare the situation between Japan and England.
In England, a ban on single-use plastic straws and stirrers has come into effect. The government made it illegal for companies to sell or supply those items. People in England use about 4.7 billion plastic straws and 316 million plastic stirrers every year. Environmentalists have welcomed the ban and called for further restrictions on other single-use items.

Class   No.   Name

30　We would like to have a debate session about this topic in our class. Please get ready to deliver your presentation next week.

Best,

David Adger

The Department of Language & Culture

(301 words)

Questions （目標2分）

1. Takuro thinks 　1　.
   ① all restaurants should stop providing plastic straws
   ② the current situation regarding the use of single-use plastics is not satisfactory
   ③ we may be able to invent alternative products in the future
   ④ we should live without plastic products

2. One **fact** stated in Takuro's article is that 　2　.
   ① it is important to reduce plastic waste
   ② now is the time when we should change our lifestyles
   ③ paper straws are now used in some restaurant chains in Japan
   ④ people cannot live without plastic products

3. Who thinks it is a good idea to compare the situation between Japan and England?
   　3　
   ① People in Japan.　　　　　　② Takuro.
   ③ Takuro's classmates.　　　　④ Takuro's professor.

4. What would you research to help Takuro prepare his presentation for the next class?
   　4　
   ① Further restrictions against plastic products in England.
   ② How the environmentalists should solve the current issues.
   ③ How many kinds of single-use plastic products there are in Japan.
   ④ Other single-use plastic products that will be banned in Japan.

Lesson 7

対応試験

CEFR A2

英検®準2級 第4部A

目標2分55秒（95 wpm）

281語÷ ___ 秒×60= ___ wpm

From: Peter Levine <petrus-levine@ymail.com>

To: Adam Moreau <adam-lepetitprince@ymail.com>

Date: October 10

Subject: Our travel itinerary

Hi, Adam!

How have you been doing?　It's been almost a year since we last met.　Yes, time flies.　My family is really missing you and your family.　My wife is looking forward to meeting your daughter again.　Is she five years old now?　Then she is about the same age as our younger son.

Winter is coming and it will turn cold soon, so we are planning to travel to Australia this winter.　Would you like to join us?　It may be a good idea to travel overseas together and enjoy the sunshine and warmer climate there.　The seasons are reversed in the Southern Hemisphere, so when it is winter in Europe and North America, it is summer in Australia.　Interestingly, however, the words are not reversed.　Winter in Australia is from June to August and summer in Australia falls between December and February.　People in Australia also call the warm season "summer" and the cold season "winter."

Let's go to the best beach in Australia!　According to the 2020 Traveladvisor Travelers' Choice Awards, Manly Beach in Sydney has been named the best in Australia.　Snorkeling is the most popular activity there.　We have a chance to see some of the unique marine life of Australia.　Also, we can rent a bike and enjoy beautiful beaches and coastal views.　After enjoying cycling, let's shop and have dinner at the shopping street near the beach.　There are a lot of choices for places to eat.　If this is your first visit to Sydney, we should try the seafood there!　I bet you'll like it!

Best,

Peter

(281 words)

Questions （目標 2 分）

1. Peter met Adam [1].
   ① for the first time in a year
   ② just a few years before
   ③ last August
   ④ nearly one year ago

2. Peter's younger son [2].
   ① is about the same age as his daughter
   ② is about the same height as Adam's daughter
   ③ is about as old as Adam's daughter
   ④ is older than Adam's sister

3. The reason why Peter's family is planning to visit Australia this winter is that [3].
   ① they have wanted to go there for a long time
   ② they want to enjoy the warmer climate of Australia
   ③ they want to invite Adam's family to the Southern Hemisphere
   ④ they want to spend their vacation in a cool place

4. Manly Beach in Sydney [4].
   ① gives people a chance to see marine life which is unique to Australia
   ② has the largest shopping mall in Australia
   ③ is said to be the best beach in the world
   ④ is the best place to enjoy surfing

Lesson
8

対応試験

CEFR A2
共通テスト第3問B

目標 3 分10秒 （95 wpm）
302語÷ ___ 秒×60＝ ___ wpm

You found the following article in a tourist magazine.

Junishi: The Hidden Aspects of the Japanese Zodiac
Eric Martin

Have you heard about *junishi*? It is the generic term for the Japanese zodiac signs taken from the old Chinese calendar.   When Buddhism arrived in Japan in the middle of the sixth century, Japanese people at that time eagerly imported innovative ideas and systems from China.   The Chinese calendar was followed by Buddhism.   It is said that this is probably the origin of the zodiac calendar in Japan.

In modern times, Japan uses the Gregorian calendar, which is the solar calendar used in most of the world.   However, the twelve zodiac signs introduced from the old Chinese calendar are very much present in Japanese culture.   A typical example of this is seen on New Year's postcards.   A lot of Japanese people send them to their relatives, friends, or coworkers.   This is like the Western custom of sending Christmas cards.   If you look at a New Year's postcard, you will find a cute zodiac design for the new year on it.

Also, you can find the twelve zodiac signs on Japanese clay bells, which are Japanese local toys made of clay.   Some Japanese clay bells are shaped like zodiac animals and they are a traditional charm against bad luck.   Buying these bells is a traditional event for Japanese people during the year-end and New Year periods.   Different regions have their own local designs.   Since they are not very expensive, a lot of tourists from abroad buy them as souvenirs.

The Japanese zodiac signs are directly derived from the Chinese ones.   The only difference is that the last animal is a boar in Japan, but a pig in China.   These signs are also used in other Asian countries, but they are different from country to country.   So you can enjoy cultural differences with them!

(302 words)

Class   No.   Name

Questions （目標2分）

1. Put the following things related to the Japanese zodiac (① ～ ④) into the order in which they are mentioned in the article. 　 1 　→ 　 2 　→ 　 3 　→ 　 4

   ① Clay bells

   ② New Year's postcards

   ③ The import of the Chinese calendar

   ④ The zodiac signs and their cultural differences

2. Japanese clay bells shaped like zodiac animals are traditionally 　 5 　.

   ① a good present for high school students

   ② a local design of a certain region

   ③ a protection from evil spirits

   ④ a purchase only during the New Year period

3. Japan's zodiac signs 　 6 　.

   ① are based on the Chinese ones, but one of the animals is different

   ② have their origin in the Chinese zodiac signs and the animals are all the same

   ③ originated in China and are also used in most of the world

   ④ started in Japan and were exported to other countries

4. From this article, you learn that 　 7 　.

   ① the Chinese zodiac calendar is popular not only in Japan but also in other Asian countries

   ② the Chinese zodiac signs follow the Japanese ones and share some features

   ③ the Japanese calendar is now based on the lunar calendar imported from China

   ④ the Japanese zodiac signs came from China and have become established in Japanese culture

Is Technology "Stealing" Our Jobs?

    Have you ever thought about jobs disappearing? Some people raise their eyebrows at the efficiency of AI (artificial intelligence), and others are afraid that it will take a lot of jobs away from human beings. Is it true that jobs will disappear and people will lose
5　their jobs?

    The answer seems to be "yes." In fact, some jobs are no longer needed as technology advances and new things are invented. For example, there were elevator operators in the past. The operator controlled the elevator when it went up and down, and he or she opened and closed the elevator doors. Once elevators became automated, this job
10　was no longer needed.

    New technology is not always welcomed with open arms, not only in modern times but historically as well. During the Industrial Revolution, many people were afraid that they could not match machines. As a result, there were workers destroying industrial machinery for fear of being deprived of their jobs. However, is technology
15　development really bad for us?

    According to a report from MIT in 2017, AI will create as many new jobs as it will eliminate. When jobs are eliminated by technology development, new ones will typically appear in other places. The report lists new jobs, like that of "empathy trainer" for AI devices. We cannot understand what this job is for now, but in the
20　future, this job might become as common as that of a teacher or any other jobs that now exist as a matter of course. Also, being a "YouTuber" is now one of the most popular jobs among kids, although it didn't exist 20 years ago.

    What we need to understand now is that AI is intended to cut out boring and troublesome parts of what we do today in our jobs. Thanks to AI and new technologies,
25　we will be able to focus on more complex and creative tasks.

(320 words)

Questions （目標2分）

1. Why do some people fear AI?　　1

　① They think that it will create new jobs that don't exist now.

　② They think that it will help to increase the number of jobs.

　③ They think that it will help to reduce the number of people out of work.

　④ They think that it will make many jobs unnecessary.

2. An elevator operator's job　2 .

　① became unnecessary when elevators were automated

　② is a good example of how technology has made progress

　③ is regarded as one of the jobs that will continue in the future

　④ turned out to be necessary when elevators became automated

3. During the Industrial Revolution, many people　3 .

　① believed that machines would perform poorly at work

　② rebelled against the government and tried to make a new society

　③ welcomed the new technology and admired the efficiency brought by it

　④ were hostile to the new technology that might replace human work

4. According to the report from MIT in 2017,　4 .

　① more jobs that are familiar to us will be created

　② old jobs will disappear, but new jobs will be created

　③ some current jobs, such as those of YouTubers, did not exist 20 years ago

　④ the jobs we cannot understand now will be eliminated

Lesson
10

対応試験

CEFR A2
共通テスト第3問B

目標3分20秒 (95 wpm)
316語÷ □ 秒×60= □ wpm

You found the following story written by a Japanese man in a wedding magazine.

My Friend's Wedding in England

On March 3, 2018, I attended a wedding ceremony in Malmesbury, England.　I was very happy to hear that my British friend, Andy, was getting married to Hilary, and I was excited to attend their wedding.　This was the very first time that I would attend a wedding in a foreign country.

When I arrived in London at 6 a.m. after coming all the way from Osaka, I found the town was covered with snow!　I got on a local train for Swindon, where Andy would pick me up.　The trains after mine were all canceled due to the heavy snow. I was very lucky, because if I had missed the train, I couldn't have attended the wedding.

Andy picked me up at Swindon Station and drove for half an hour from there to our hotel in Malmesbury.　The hotel where we stayed for the wedding was called the Old Bell Hotel, and it was said to be one of the oldest hotels in England.　At night, I attended a party where only same-sex friends of the groom got together. Of course, a party of the same kind was held for the bride in another place.

The next day, the wedding ceremony was held at the church near the hotel. Then, there was a reception party at the cottage and we enjoyed a wonderful meal, talking with each other.　We had a great party that night which was called the after-party.　At the party, we danced to live music with many friends of the bride and groom.

The next afternoon, we had another party at Andy's parents' house.　This was the last party.　The two families got together and they had a lot of conversation as if they were one big family.　At the end of the party, we saw off the bride and groom as they left for their honeymoon.

(316 words)

Questions（目標2分）

1. Put the following places（①〜④）into the order in which the writer moved among them. ⎡ 1 ⎤ → ⎡ 2 ⎤ → ⎡ 3 ⎤ → ⎡ 4 ⎤

① London

② Malmesbury

③ Osaka

④ Swindon

2. The writer ⎡ 5 ⎤ .

① attended a wedding ceremony abroad for the first time

② was getting married to a friend in Britain

③ was very excited to invite a friend in Britain to his wedding

④ was very happy to attend a meeting held in Britain

3. The writer ⎡ 6 ⎤ .

① attended the parties as a friend of the bride

② enjoyed the party only for men on the night of his arrival

③ invited a lot of his friends to a dance party

④ missed the train and was picked up by his friend at the station

4. The writer attended ⎡ 7 ⎤ in total.

① two parties

② three parties

③ four parties

④ five parties

Lesson

11

 対応 試験

CEFR B1

GTEC® パートC
英検® 2級 第3部BC

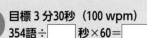

目標 3 分30秒 （100 wpm）
354語÷ ☐ 秒×60= ☐ wpm

What do the colors of countries' flags mean? The colors are important factors to distinguish one flag from others and help us remember what country or organization each flag represents. In addition to that, the colors convey certain messages to us.

Different colors have different meanings. It is generally said that black means power
5 and authority and white means purity and innocence. However, the colors used in the flags of countries or organizations do not always mean the same thing. The colors of flags sometimes have different meanings, depending on the historical and cultural backgrounds of the countries or organizations.

Let's look at the example of the Australian Aboriginal flag. The flag was first flown
10 on National Aboriginal Day in Adelaide in 1971. Now, it is recognized as one of the official flags of Australia by the government. The flag is a colored rectangle divided horizontally into halves. The upper half is black and the lower half is red. The circle at the center of the flag is yellow. According to the designer of the flag, Harold Thomas, the black represents the Aboriginal people of Australia, the yellow circle
15 means the sun, and the red represents the red earth.

Take a look at the national flag of Japan. There is a red circle at the center of the flag, and it represents the rising sun. On the other hand, red may remind people in other countries of blood or wars. Some people say that is why red is not used in the flag of the United Nations or those of many other international organizations.

20 Different colors give us different information, and sometimes people interpret colors differently. You may have noticed the different interpretations of the color red in the Aboriginal flag and the Japanese flag. The colors of their flags play an important role in establishing the images of the countries or organizations. The next time you see a flag of a country, it may be a good chance to think about the meanings of the colors of the
25 flag. You will get important messages from them because colors are powerful sources of information.

(354 words)

Questions （目標2分）

1. How are the colors of flags helpful for us? ☐1
   ① They help us convey messages.
   ② They help us identify the flags.
   ③ They help us remember the general images of colors.
   ④ They help us tell the different designs apart.

2. What is special about the colors of countries' flags? ☐2
   ① All of them have particular meanings unique to each country.
   ② Some of them are based on people's common knowledge.
   ③ Some of them are decided, based on countries' history or culture.
   ④ They are always based on basic meanings of colors.

3. What does the color red in the Australian Aboriginal flag stand for? ☐3
   ① It stands for being against war.
   ② It stands for blood and warfare.
   ③ It stands for the red land.
   ④ It stands for the sun rising from the east.

4. What is this passage mainly about? ☐4
   ① How the colors of the national flag affect people's way of thinking.
   ② What you can learn from the colors of flags.
   ③ When people started to use the colors for flags.
   ④ Why people are interested in the colors of flags.

Lesson
12

対応試験

CEFR B1
共通テスト第4問

目標4分5秒（100 wpm）
409語÷ □ 秒×60＝ □ wpm

You are doing research on the world economy. You have found an article and an opinion about it.

Burgernomics: The Big Mac index and the purchasing power of a currency

by Martin Gibson

August 23, 2020

Purchasing power parity is an economic theory which states that the currency exchange rate can be determined by the ratio of the purchasing power between two currencies. Based on this theory, the Big Mac index was invented by *The Economist* in 1986. This index has been used to compare the values of currencies by using the price of a Big Mac as a benchmark.

In theory, the price of a Big Mac reflects many local economic factors, from the cost of the ingredients to the cost of production and advertising. Therefore, a lot of economists consider the Big Mac index to be a reasonable indicator of the actual purchasing power of a currency and a good basis for determining the validity of exchange rates.

The graph below shows the price of a Big Mac in each country in U.S. dollars as of January 2020. In the graph, we can say that the currencies of the eight countries below the United States are undervalued against the U.S. dollar.

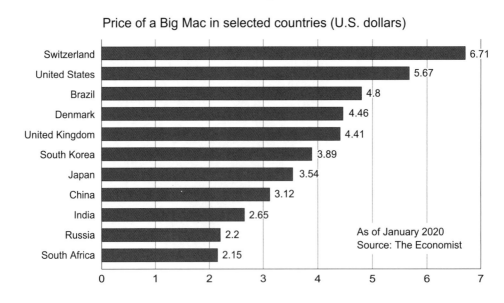

Price of a Big Mac in selected countries (U.S. dollars)

Switzerland	6.71
United States	5.67
Brazil	4.8
Denmark	4.46
United Kingdom	4.41
South Korea	3.89
Japan	3.54
China	3.12
India	2.65
Russia	2.2
South Africa	2.15

As of January 2020
Source: The Economist

20   A Big Mac is basically the same sandwich anywhere in the world even though it is never exported in its final form.   So we may be able to say that labor in Japan is less expensive than that in Switzerland by comparing the price of a Big Mac in both countries in the graph.

We can also refer to the Starbucks Index and compare it with the Big Mac Index.

Price of a Starbucks Latte (U.S. dollars)

Rank	Country / Region	Price (USD)	Rank	Country / Region	Price (USD)
1	Denmark	$6.05	6	Norway	$5.14
2	Switzerland	$5.94	7	Hong Kong	$4.60
3	Finland	$5.40	8	Singapore	$4.50
4	Macao	$5.21	9	Germany	$4.39
5	Luxembourg	$5.18	10	Russia	$4.35

Source: Finder 2019

Opinion on "Burgernomics: The Big Mac index and the purchasing power of a
25   currency"   **by Y. T.**

October 10, 2020

I wonder whether the Big Mac index can measure the economic power of each country accurately.   The total price of a Big Mac will also be affected by tariff rates, consumption tax rates, and the economic condition of each country.   Therefore, it
30   will be different among countries and will not reflect overall relative currency values.   Moreover, there are cultural differences.   McDonald's is a fast food restaurant for ordinary people in many countries, but it is sometimes regarded as a restaurant for rich people or tourists in other countries.   This is not taken into account in the Big Mac index.

(409 words)

Questions （目標 2 分30秒）

1. Both Martin Gibson and Y. T. show us   1 .

① areas where you can purchase a Big Mac at the lowest price

② that the comparison of Big Mac prices in different countries is beneficial

③ views of the Big Mac index

④ why many experts wonder if the Big Mac index is accurate

2. Which best completes the description below? $\boxed{2}$

> · $\boxed{\text{A}}$ is ranked higher than $\boxed{\text{B}}$ in both indexes.
> · The currency in $\boxed{\text{C}}$ is overvalued against the U.S. dollar, according to Martin's article.
> · $\boxed{\text{A}}$ is ranked higher than $\boxed{\text{C}}$ in the Starbucks index.
> · $\boxed{\text{D}}$ is listed below $\boxed{\text{B}}$ in the Big Mac index.

① A：Denmark　　B：China　　　C：Germany　　　D：Russia

② A：Denmark　　B：Russia　　　C：Switzerland　　D：South Africa

③ A：Russia　　　B：Denmark　　C：Switzerland　　D：South Africa

④ A：Russia　　　B：Switzerland　C：United Kingdom　D：Norway

3. Martin Gibson states that the Big Mac index $\boxed{\text{3a}}$, and Y. T. states that it $\boxed{\text{3b}}$. (Choose a different option for each box.)

① can be a reliable way to judge the accuracy of currency exchange rates

② compares the price of a Big Mac in each area of a country

③ determines the profit range in many countries

④ is not always appropriate for evaluating the value of a currency

⑤ will help to improve the world economic condition

4. Based on the information from both passages, you are going to write a report for homework. The best title for your report would be "$\boxed{4}$."

① The Advantages and Disadvantages of the Big Mac Index

② The Big Mac Index: Expert Analysis and Its Evidence

③ The Growing Popularity of the Big Mac Index in Different Countries

④ The Differences and Similarities between the Big Mac Index and Purchasing Power Parity

スピーキング・トレーナー

◯)) 本文を音読しよう☐　　373語÷ ☐ 秒×60= ☐ wpm

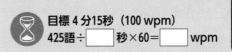

You are writing a review of the story, "Oliver's English Camp Experience," in class.

Oliver's English Camp Experience

The summer after my freshman year of university, I was chosen as a volunteer English teacher for a junior high school English camp in Spain. For the first time, I had the opportunity to experience the classroom from the other side of the teacher's desk. My responsibility was simple: in two weeks, to turn sixteen junior high school students into confident English speakers. I was looking forward to the opportunity to share my knowledge with the students and tell them the joy of communicating in English. I thought every student would be eager to learn and attentive to my every word.

Unfortunately, however, in my class was a boy named Alonso, who thought class was a good time to train his basketball skills by tossing plastic bottles into the trash can from his desk. I was also in charge of a girl named Carmen, who thought I wouldn't notice her reading cookbooks all day. The only questions I got from the students were "When's lunch break?" and "Why are you giving us homework?" During just ten minutes of the beginning of the class, two things hit me: Alonso's plastic bottle and the realization that teaching was hard.

I thought about what I should do to encourage my students to try speaking in public. I didn't know the answer, but I really wanted them to know how fun it is to express their favorite things. Every day for two weeks, I searched for creative ways to teach my students. I encouraged Alonso to talk about effective training skills for basketball; I helped Carmen speak on her love for cooking.

I was on the other side of the teacher's desk, but I didn't stop learning. I was learning how to interact more effectively with students and how to be a better teacher. I once thought that being an adult meant knowing all the answers. However, even teachers have much to learn.

By the time the camp was over, the students came to enjoy learning English. After I came back to my homeland, I received a postcard from Alonso.

Dear Oliver,
I'm sorry for the way I behaved at the camp. At first, I was not

Class　　No.　　Name

Active
Practical Reading 完成編　13−1

interested in learning English at all.   Later, when you taught us
English enthusiastically, I realized how much fun learning
English was and I regretted throwing plastic bottles at you
during class.
  So long,
  Alonso

I am confident that the students enjoyed learning something new from my lessons.   And even as their teacher, I learned and had fun, too.

(425 words)

Story Review	Title:
	Oliver's English Camp Experience

Outline

Beginning	Middle	Ending
1	2 → 3	4

Main characters

- Oliver tried to [5].
- Alonso didn't like Oliver's class at first, [6].

Your opinions

Oliver hoped that his students [7].   I liked how Oliver worked hard and eventually made his students happy with his lessons.

Who is most likely to find this story interesting?

8

35

Questions （目標3分）

1. Put the following events into the order in which they happened. [1] ～ [4]
   ① Oliver and his students learned a lot from the English camp.
   ② Oliver encouraged his students to express themselves.
   ③ Oliver had the opportunity to teach English to junior high school students in Spain.
   ④ Some students were not willing to learn English and felt bored.

2. Choose the best option for [5].
   ① do his best to attract the students' attention
   ② introduce to the students how interesting studying abroad was
   ③ make every effort to improve his lessons until the end of the camp
   ④ tell the students how to be good English teachers

3. Choose the best option for [6].
   ① because he got a lot of homework in Oliver's lessons
   ② but later he got interested in learning English
   ③ even though he was originally very interested in speaking English
   ④ so he tried to improve his English by expressing himself about basketball, his favorite sport

4. Choose the best option for [7].
   ① would enjoy talking about what they like in English
   ② would have an opportunity to speak English in public
   ③ would have much to learn when they became adults
   ④ would like to be better at teaching English

5. Choose the best option for [8].
   ① People who want to become a teacher in the near future.
   ② People who want to know why they have to study at school.
   ③ People who want to remember their own childhood experiences with friends.
   ④ People who want to understand the relationship between children and adults.

スピーキング・トレーナー
◁)) 本文を音読しよう□   425語÷ □ 秒×60= □ wpm

Lesson

14

対応試験

CEFR B1
共通テスト第6問A

目標4分10秒（100 wpm）
421語÷□秒×60=□wpm

You are preparing for a presentation about the IoT (Internet of Things). You have found an article about home automation. You are going to read the article and make a poster for the presentation.

Home Automation

In today's world, our lives are deeply rooted in technology. It has a positive effect on the way we live, work and even socialize. Just a little more than 30 years ago, there were no smartphones and no Internet in practically every home. In the 1980s, you would see people using public pay phones. It was like a different world! Though the time between then and now seems to be relatively short, sometimes the development of technology is taken for granted and we forget how integrated into technology our lives are. Can you imagine life without the Internet or smartphones?

The combination of smartphones and the Internet has changed the world, and we are just now seeing the beginning of another big change in our personal environment. It is referred to as home automation. This smart home system includes the automation and control of various electronic systems in a house, for example, smart bulbs and smart vacuum cleaners. Smart home technology is built on the idea that electronic systems at home should be connected so that they are able to communicate with and affect each other.

Thanks to smart home technology, our lives will become more and more convenient. For example, if you use a smart light bulb, you can turn the light on and off with an app on your smartphone. This may not sound like a great leap forward, but other great products that are based on the same basic technology and make our homes more comfortable have been and are being developed. For example, smart thermostats can now control home heating and cooling appliances without human intervention.

Another of the good things about smart home technologies is that they are better at managing power usage. Heating and cooling costs will be cut down if you use smart thermostats. They can control the temperature precisely and they only heat and cool the areas that are being used. Also, they are programmed to be more adaptive to your environment. This not only saves money but also reduces your

Class　　No.　　Name

home's carbon footprint, and you will be encouraged to become more aware of your energy consumption.

35 　　　Home automation offers us both improved energy efficiency and broader functionality at home.　We should learn how to use smart devices because they will only become smarter as time goes by.　Everything at home, from cleaning to heating, will soon be automated.　What do you think a smart home will look like ten years from now?　We can expect further developments in home automation.

(421 words)

Home Automation

Technology positively influences ...
- lifestyle.　　　　　　・working style.　　　　・ 1 .

Home Automation ...
- 2 .
- includes smart bulbs and smart vacuum cleaners.
- is based on the idea of connecting home electronic systems with each other

Examples of smart home technology	
· **Smart light bulbs** Light bulbs that can be turned on and off with an app. 💡This may not seem like a great technological advance.	· **Smart thermostats** Thermostats that can control air-conditioning systems without human intervention. 💡This product 3 .

Advantages of smart home technologies
· 4
· 5
· They reduce carbon footprints at home.
· They will automate nearly everything at home in the future.

Main points: _____ 6 _____

Questions （目標3分）

1. Choose the best option for ☐ 1 ☐ on your poster.
   ① socialism　　　② socializing　　　③ social issues　　　④ sociology

2. Choose the best option for ☐ 2 ☐ on your poster.
   ① is based on a big change in our personal environment
   ② is one of the major changes taking place in our personal environment
   ③ has been a wonderful invention for our personal life
   ④ has caused the combination of various smart technologies

3. Choose the best option for ☐ 3 ☐ on your poster.
   ① is based on the same basic technology as smart light bulbs
   ② is developed for turning on and off air conditioners with an app
   ③ is made for electric communication systems
   ④ is seen as a big leap toward human intervention

4. Choose the best items for ☐ 4 ☐ and ☐ 5 ☐.　(The order does not matter.)
   ① They are programmed to make the home environment more suitable for the residents.
   ② They cut down the cost of making home automation possible.
   ③ They provide better management of power usage.
   ④ They save energy at home in order to sell it to companies.

5. This article mainly discusses ☐ 6 ☐.
   ① the advantages and disadvantages of using home automation systems compared to using other systems
   ② the reasons why people started to use home automation, and why it has gained popularity
   ③ the similarities and differences between home automation and the Internet of Things, and the benefits of the two
   ④ what home automation is like and what benefits smart devices may bring to us

スピーキング・トレーナー
本文を音読しよう☐　421語÷☐秒×60＝☐wpm

You are the editor of your school newspaper. You have been asked to provide comments on an article about manga written by an Australian student named Amelia.

Manga

[1]   Have you heard the word "manga"? It means Japanese comic books. A lot of people in Japan enjoy reading them. Manga, which include pictures and texts, have traditionally been an essential part of Japanese popular culture.

[2]   It is said that the Japanese word "manga" was first used late in the 18th century. Later, in 1814, the *Hokusai Manga*, which is one of the most famous works of Katsushika Hokusai (1760-1849), was published. It became popular not only in Japan but also overseas. However, it was a kind of picture book and different from the manga we think of now.

[3]   After World War II, manga which were based on the stories of *kamishibai*, or picture story shows, developed rapidly and spread over a lot of media types, including weekly magazines. Since then, manga have become more and more widespread in Japan.

[4]   [A   ] We should mention Tezuka Osamu when we talk about why manga are popular now. [B   ] He is considered to be "the god of manga" for his role in the development of what are now known as story manga. A television series was created, based on his already established manga, *Astro Boy* (*Mighty Atom*). Its popularity was not limited to existing readers of the original manga. [C   ] Even today, Astro Boy can be found on T-shirts, key rings, bags, posters and thousands of other goods. It was Tezuka who created the basis for the combination of manga, anime and media. [D   ]

[5]   On this background, manga have become universally popular. In Japan, men and women of all ages enjoy reading various kinds of manga at home——and even at school! They also read manga in public places, such as in trains and in the waiting rooms of hospitals. Manga cafés have been increasing in number in the last few years. They offer many shelves of manga of various genres and a quiet space to read them for an hourly fee.

[6]   Manga have many interesting features, and they are a part of Japanese

popular culture.　Should people around the world have more access to them?　Yes, of course!　We should all jump into this unique culture and enjoy it.

(373 words)

Questions （目標 2 分30秒）

1. Amelia's article mainly discusses ⬚1⬚ .
   ① how manga is superior to other parts of Japanese culture
   ② the invention of new types of manga in foreign countries
   ③ the nature and place of manga in Japanese popular culture
   ④ the use of manga for cultural and educational purposes

2. Amelia's intention in Paragraphs [2], [3] and [4] is probably to ⬚2⬚ .
   ① describe manga's historical development in Japan
   ② discuss the possibility of introducing manga as traditional Japanese art
   ③ express concerns about the popularity of manga in Japan
   ④ introduce some contributions of manga to people of different ages

3. You found additional information related to this topic and want to suggest that Amelia add the sentence below to her article.　Where would the sentence best fit among the four locations marked [　A　], [　B　], [　C　] and [　D　] in Paragraph [4]?　⬚3⬚

   It introduced manga to a whole new generation of readers and expanded the manga market to other fields.
   ① [　A　]　　② [　B　]　　③ [　C　]　　④ [　D　]

4. Amelia implies that ⬚4⬚ .
   ① people from abroad cannot enjoy manga very much
   ② people in Japan should explain to the world how attractive manga are
   ③ people in other countries should have fewer opportunities to enjoy manga
   ④ people all over the world can understand and enjoy manga

スピーキング・トレーナー
🔊 本文を音読しよう▢　　373語÷▢秒×60＝▢wpm

Lesson
16

対応試験

CEFR B1
GTEC® パートC
英検® 2級 第3部BC

目標 4 分10秒 (100 wpm)
421語÷ [　] 秒×60= [　] wpm

Mark Haub is a professor of human nutrition at Kansas State University. In 2010, he embarked on a 10-week journey to a land where no fitness professionals had ever been. Mark decided to prove once and for all that weight loss was simply a matter of calorie intake and nothing else. There were some diet methods that claimed calorie-counting

5 was irrelevant and unnecessary for the sake of weight loss, and that watching what we eat was important. However, Mark tried to disprove those diet methods. In order to do that, he decided only to eat foods that were considered junk foods. These foods included potato chips, chocolate cookies, and cakes with creams, such as Twinkies.

For 10 weeks, Mark ate one of these junk foods every three hours, instead of daily

10 healthy food. In addition to the junk foods, he ate a serving of vegetables, a protein drink, and a multivitamin every day to help fight against any potential vitamin and mineral deficiencies. His calorie intake was approximately 1,800 kilocalories per day, though it would have taken 2,600 kilocalories to maintain his weight. This created an 800-kilocalorie deficit per day.

15 Did the Twinkie diet work? Surprisingly, it worked! By the end of the 10 weeks, Mark was able to lose 27 pounds. You might think the diet is not healthy, but the amount of his "bad" cholesterol dropped by 20 percent and the amount of his "good" cholesterol increased by 20 percent. The percentage of his body fat dropped from 33.4 to 24.9 percent. Mark showed that weight loss is simply about eating fewer calories.

20 According to his study, what counts is caloric intake only. He proved that just restricting calories is important.

Does only the amount of calories matter for weight loss, and is the quality of what we eat not important? Or, should we do as Mark did if we want to lose weight? Mark is not recommending his Twinkie diet as a weight-loss plan for others. "I wish I could

25 state clearly whether this method is good or not," he said. "I'm not confident enough to do that. That frustrates a lot of people. One side says I'm irresponsible. The diet is unhealthy, but the data doesn't say that." His data may not say that junk food is unhealthy. However, considering that about two-thirds of the population in the U.S. is suffering from being overweight, we should think more about whether junk food is

30 really healthy in the long run and what a healthy diet is all about.

(421 words)

Class 　　 No. 　　 Name

Questions （目標2分30秒）

1. What did Prof. Mark Haub decide to prove in 2010?　[　1　]
   ① That no fitness professionals have ever been on a 10-week journey.
   ② That nothing else is more important than taking calories to stay healthy.
   ③ That the amount of calorie intake is important for losing weight.
   ④ That weight gain and loss are affected by many things besides caloric intake.

2. What did Mark do in order to lose weight?　[　2　]
   ① He fought against vitamin and mineral deficiencies by eating junk foods.
   ② He mainly ate a serving of vegetables, a protein drink, and a multivitamin every day.
   ③ He mainly ate junk foods such as Twinkies and limited his calorie intake.
   ④ He seriously counted the calories he took in and ate junk foods such as hamburgers.

3. What was the result of Mark's Twinkie diet?　[　3　]
   ① He succeeded in losing 27 pounds by the end of the 10 weeks and stayed healthy.
   ② It did not work because he gained weight and became unhealthy.
   ③ It worked well only for Mark losing weight, but he became unhealthy in the end.
   ④ The amount of his bad cholesterol increased by 20% and the amount of his body fat dropped by 20%.

4. In the end, what is Mark's opinion about the Twinkie diet? <u>4</u>

① He does not recommend the Twinkie diet and he is not still sure whether it is good or bad.

② He does not recommend the Twinkie diet, based on his data.

③ He recommends the Twinkie diet, but he is not sure if it works in the long run.

④ He recommends the Twinkie diet to everyone as a new weight-loss plan.

5. What is this passage mainly about? <u>5</u>

① How the Twinkie diet has become widespread.

② The only thing we should do in order not to suffer from being overweight.

③ What Prof. Mark Haub revealed through his diet program, and remaining questions.

④ Why Prof. Mark Haub needed to lose weight, and what he did.

In class, everyone wrote reports based on the two graphs below.　Chris and Kazuma are going to make a presentation based on their own reports.

The topic of these graphs is self-driving cars.　Contrary to popular belief, there are still a number of people who remain uncomfortable with self-driving cars.

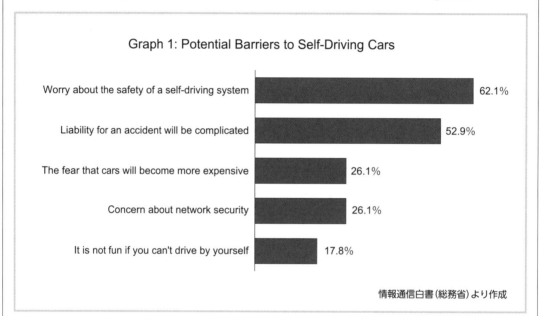

Graph 1: Potential Barriers to Self-Driving Cars

Worry about the safety of a self-driving system	62.1%
Liability for an accident will be complicated	52.9%
The fear that cars will become more expensive	26.1%
Concern about network security	26.1%
It is not fun if you can't drive by yourself	17.8%

情報通信白書（総務省）より作成

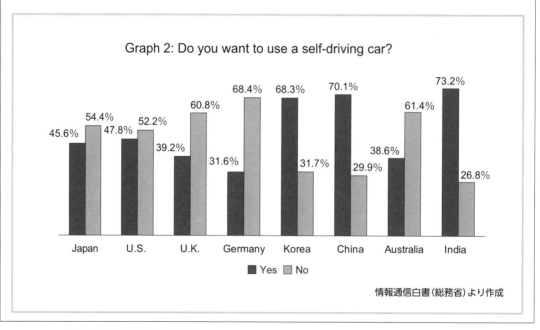

Graph 2: Do you want to use a self-driving car?

	Yes	No
Japan	45.6%	54.4%
U.S.	47.8%	52.2%
U.K.	39.2%	60.8%
Germany	31.6%	68.4%
Korea	68.3%	31.7%
China	70.1%	29.9%
Australia	38.6%	61.4%
India	73.2%	26.8%

情報通信白書（総務省）より作成

Class　　No.　　Name

Active
Practical Reading 完成編

Chris Coleman

What comes to mind when you think about self-driving cars? Two advantages come to my mind. First, I associate them with having more freedom. Not having to focus on driving means that people have free time for doing other things in a car. Another positive aspect is that the burden on freight drivers is relieved. For example, truck drivers would not feel stressed and exhausted because they would not have to drive their trucks by themselves anymore.

Though self-driving technology is still in progress, it is becoming increasingly common and could dramatically change our transportation system, and even our economy and society. However, contrary to my expectation, Graph 1 says that a lot of people still worry about self-driving cars. People seem to be especially interested in technological matters. Since they do not trust the self-driving technology, they worry about who will be responsible if a self-driving car causes an accident.

Those who are concerned about self-driving cars do not know much about the latest developments of self-driving cars, and they should learn more about the benefits of them. Automaker companies should promote self-driving cars in order to get people more interested in them.

Kazuma Kitamura

Currently, in Japan, fully-autonomous cars are not available. Also, it may still be a little difficult to imagine that self-driving cars will be seen often anywhere in the world. As you can see from Graph 2, many people in Japan are hesitant to use self-driving cars, so it is unlikely that self-driving cars will become usual soon. I was shocked to see that many people in Japan and other countries, which are focusing on developing self-driving cars, don't want to ride in them. They are probably worried about their safety at the moment.

In addition to the concern about the safety of self-driving cars, there is another problem to get over. If they were sold in Japan, some traffic laws would need to be changed.　At the moment, Japanese laws require a human driver when a self-driving car is used.　The human driver should always be ready to intervene and take control of the car when necessary.

　　Toyota, one of the world's largest automakers, aims to realize the "Level 4" automated car in a few years.　"Level 4" means the car can perform all of the driving tasks in some driving situations, though not all.　Therefore, I think some cars in Japan can be driverless in the next several years.　I'm looking forward to a future with self-driving cars, and I will keep my eyes on the trends of this industry, especially how to promote them.

(523 words)

Presentation draft:

The Present and the Future of Self-Driving Cars
Advantages of self-driving cars: 1. ☐ 1
2. They can remove ☐ 2 from freight drivers.
Present
┃...Many people ☐ 3 .
┃...Fully-autonomous cars are not available in Japan.
To realize the widespread use of self-driving cars,
• safety must be improved so that people can use them with peace of mind.
• laws must be changed ☐ 4 .
Future
...“Level 4” automated cars are planned to be realized within a few years
└→“level”: Self-driving cars ☐ 5 .
Theme for our future research: ☐ 6

Questions （目標3分）

1. Choose the best option for ☐ 1 .
　① They can accelerate technological development.
　② They can free drivers from having to focus on driving.
　③ They can free the driver from liability for accidents.
　④ They can dramatically change the economy and society.

2. Choose the best option for ☐2☐.

① essential skills for driving

② inevitable accidents

③ physical and mental fatigue

④ the need for their work

3. Choose the best option for ☐3☐.

① believe that self-driving cars are safer than traditional cars

② cannot afford to buy self-driving cars

③ doubt the safety of self-driving cars

④ want to enjoy driving by themselves

4. Choose the best option for ☐4☐.

① because they don't take into account the existence of self-driving cars

② to allow car companies to develop fully-autonomous vehicles

③ to completely eliminate the need for human drivers

④ so that drivers can focus on driving all the time

5. Choose the best option for ☐5☐.

① are classified, depending on their automation level

② are eagerly awaited by people around the world

③ might deprive people of the joy of driving

④ will push our economy to a higher level

6. Choose the best title for ☐6☐.

① A New Transportation System for Self-Driving Cars

② Differences between Autonomous Cars in Japan and Other Countries

③ How Car Advertising Has Changed and How It Will Change

④ How Toyota Produces Autonomous Cars

Lesson

18

対応試験

CEFR B1

共通テスト第5問

⏳ 目標 4 分30秒 （110 wpm）
496語÷☐秒×60＝☐wpm

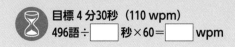

Your group is preparing a poster presentation entitled "How Kojima Became the Denim Capital," using information from the magazine article below.

In the last two decades, a city in Okayama Prefecture has become world-famous. What is the city in Western Honshu famous for? It is well known as the main
5 source of Japan's "vintage" jeans, which are of high quality and have been sold for many years. Those who are interested in denim products go to a small seaside city called Kojima, which is known as "Japan's Denim Capital."

The story of Japanese jeans started many years ago with small-scale cotton agriculture and a textile industry around Kojima. Okayama was not known for
10 indigo dyeing and textile industries. However, one single company, Maruo Clothing, which later changed its name to BIG JOHN, played an important role in making Okayama a denim mecca.

Maruo was a leader in Kojima for making school uniforms. After World War II, cotton was in short supply, so Maruo made uniforms from a cheap synthetic fiber
15 called vinylon. This went well until two big textile companies, TORAY and TEIJIN, started selling a better polyester called Tetoron. In the end, Maruo withdrew from the vinylon uniform business. In the postwar years, Maruo took contract work from a jeans shop in Tokyo to re-cut discarded old American jeans to fit Japanese bodies. After that, Maruo started to produce their own jeans. They
20 were surely much cheaper than American imports.

With the school uniform business crashing, Maruo decided to become a jeans manufacturer. At first, it was difficult for Maruo to get enough denim fabric, so Maruo sewed jeans for the Canton brand in Tokyo, not for their own brand. By 1967, however, Maruo managed to sign a contract with a company in North Carolina
25 to source B-grade rolls of denim, with which they created an original line called BIG JOHN. This brand went on to become the best-selling jeans brand in Japan through the 1970s. It even beat out the brands which originated in the U.S.: LEVI'S, Lee and Wrangler. For decades after that, Kojima acted as the design, sewing and washing base in Japan for jeans.
30 In the 1990s, other high-end brands appeared: Studio D'Artisan, Denime, EVISU,

Class　No.　Name

FULL COUNT, and WAREHOUSE.　Behind the scenes, some of them were highly dependent upon Okayama factories for sewing.　In addition, FULL COUNT worked with Kojima's denim factories to make the world's first denim made from Zimbabwe long-staple cotton.　In the beginning of the 2000s, some other companies in Kojima started to make their own high-end jeans.　These new brands turned Kojima from just a sewing base into a city known for artistic and cutting-edge denim.

In 2009, a plan to build a "Kojima Jeans Street" was launched in order to celebrate Kojima's history and brands and attract more tourists.　A special jeans-themed bus takes tourists to the street, where each of the local brands has its own shop.　To make things more fun, they even serve denim-colored blueberry ice cream.　Other companies, meanwhile, have opened a jeans museum and have been working on promoting Kojima's attractions nationwide.

(496 words)

How Kojima Became the Denim Capital

■ The History of Okayama as Japan's Denim Capital

Period	Events
Before World War II	Okayama was not known for indigo dyeing and textile industries.
During the postwar period	1 ↓
In the 1960s and 1970s	2 ↓
In the 1990s	3 ↓
From 2000 and beyond	4 ↓ 5

■ About Maruo: Changes in their business style

▶ After the war, Maruo did the following things: 6 · 7
▶ Maruo finally succeeded in 8 .

■ About Kojima in the modern age

▶ In 2009, the "Kojima Jeans Street" was started.
▶ Some jeans companies in Kojima 9 .

1. Members of your group listed important events in the development of Japan's denim capital. Put the events into the boxes ⎡ 1 ⎤ ~ ⎡ 5 ⎤ in the order that they happened.
   ① In Kojima, Maruo Clothing started a jeans-related business.
   ② Kojima became a well-known city for producing high-quality denim.
   ③ Kojima became the center for making jeans in Japan.
   ④ Kojima started its "Kojima Jeans Street," which has jeans shops for tourists.
   ⑤ Some high-end jeans brands appeared on Japan's denim scene.

2. Choose the best statements to complete the poster. (Choose two options. The order does not matter.) ⎡ 6 ⎤ · ⎡ 7 ⎤
   ① They became famous for indigo dyeing and textile industries.
   ② They created a brand-new Japanese denim brand.
   ③ They gave up making school uniforms.
   ④ They limited access to denim fabric.
   ⑤ They made a shop in Tokyo to sell Japanese domestic-made jeans.
   ⑥ They signed a contract with a jeans shop to repair old Japanese jeans.

3. Which of the following is the most appropriate for filling in the box ⎡ 8 ⎤?
   ① acting as the design, sewing and washing base in Japan for jeans
   ② being one of the best-selling jeans brands in the world
   ③ convincing a North Carolina company to send them American jeans
   ④ producing the best-selling jeans brand, BIG JOHN, in Japan through the 1970s

4. Which of the following is the most appropriate for filling in the box ⎡ 9 ⎤?
   ① are making efforts to promote jeans and the city of Kojima
   ② are opening their old factories as museums for tourists
   ③ are running buses which go around Kojima
   ④ are serving denim-colored blueberry ice cream nationwide

スピーキング・トレーナー
🔊)) 本文を音読しよう☐ 496語÷☐秒×60=☐wpm

Lesson
19

対応試験

CEFR B1

共通テスト第6問A

目標 4 分45秒 （110 wpm）
524語÷□秒×60＝□wpm

You are preparing for a group presentation on medical treatment and health for your class. You have found the article below.

Music Therapy

Since the earliest days of humankind, the power of music has been evident to us. If you like music, you probably already know it can affect your mood. Maybe you put on your favorite song to encourage yourself for an important meeting or listen to soothing music when you are relaxing at home before going to bed.

Music offers a variety of benefits and for that reason it is used as a medical treatment. Music therapy consists of different elements, such as making music, writing songs, and listening to music. Research has demonstrated the benefits of music therapy for people with depression and anxiety. While music therapy is often used to promote mental and emotional health, it also improves the quality of life for people with physical health problems.

During World War II, musicians visited a U.S. military hospital and played music to console the wounded soldiers. The soldiers who listened to the music healed more quickly. This shows that music therapy is physically effective, too. Another example can be found in nursing homes. When the residents listen to pleasant music, they want to move their body with others and eventually their physical functions improve.

People who make use of music for medical treatment are called music therapists. They are trained in fields other than music; their education often covers a wide range of clinical skills, including communication, cognitive neuroscience, and psychological disorders, as well as chronic illness and pain management. They use music therapy in a variety of ways, including having people sing along to music, meditate and relax while music is played, and conduct various exercises and movements with music.

How does music affect patients' minds and bodies? Music has various effects on the activity of a large range of brain structures. Neuroscience studies have recently revealed that listening to music can have effects on the core structures of

Class　　No.　　Name

30 emotional processing in the brain. In short, music improves patients' minds and bodies as it stimulates their brains.

Stimulating the brain with music is similar to developing a stronger heart with cardiovascular exercises. The brain is no different from any other organ, in that when it is exercised, it becomes sharper and more highly developed. Music

35 directly affects brain waves, as stronger and faster rhythms make people more alert while slower music can help people to meditate and relax. This healthy calming effect helps people to develop a positive mind state while reducing stress, which lowers blood pressure. This is why music therapy is used for rehabilitation at some hospitals.

40 What kind of music should we listen to? The choice of songs that have the desired effect is often linked to personality traits. The effect of different types of music on mood will largely depend on people's individual preferences and experiences. If you grow up with rock music, you might not find classical music uplifting. On the flipside, some people cannot bear rock music. They are more

45 likely to become wound up by it than uplifted. However, at least as a general rule, if you want to relax, you should choose songs with a slower tempo and a more predictable structure.

(524 words)

Questions (目標2分)

1. In the article, the author says music is used as a medical treatment because ⬚1⬚ .
   ① it does not change people's moods at all
   ② it has little effect on people's minds but affects their bodies
   ③ it offers various benefits such as reduction of stress
   ④ it relieves people's fear and anxiety about surgery

2. According to the article, the benefits of music therapy 　2　 .

① are clearly denied by neuroscience researchers

② are enhanced by music therapists who are trained in fields other than music

③ are observed among people with physical health problems as well as among people with mental disorders

④ are supported by a wide range of skills that music therapists have developed

3. In the article, the author says the brain is partly the same as other organs because 　3　 .

① it can calm down the heartbeat and lower blood pressure when people are listening to slower music

② it gets better by listening to music just as the heart gets stronger by exercising

③ it gets stronger through cardiovascular exercises

④ music directly affects it because stronger and faster rhythms make people more alert

4. Which of the following statements best summarizes the article? 　4　

① Music has been popular among people for a long time because it improves people's moods.

② Music has been with people for a long time, so it helps to reduce their stress.

③ Music has effects on human brains, so it works as a medical therapy.

④ Music has some benefits only when patients are properly treated by therapists.

スピーキング・トレーナー

◝)) 本文を音読しよう□　　524語÷ □ 秒×60= □ wpm

You are studying about global environmental problems.　You are going to read the following article to understand food waste problems.

In 2015, about 340 million tons of food were wasted after purchase globally, and much of it was believed to be still edible.　A large amount of fuel is used to dispose of food as garbage, which contributes to global warming.　Throwing away food not only wastes a lot of money, but it is also bad for the environment.　In addition, considering that many people in the world are suffering from starvation, it is a shame to throw away edible food.　Food waste is a big problem that needs to be solved globally.

It is said, especially in developed countries, that best-before dates contribute to the huge amount of food waste.　Researchers have found that Americans throw away billions of pounds of food every year because they falsely believe that best-before dates on package labels indicate food safety.　In other words, people are likely to think that foods that have passed their best-before dates are not safe to eat and throw them away even though they are actually still edible.　These dates have nothing to do with the risk of food poisoning.　A best-before date is not a date to indicate spoilage, nor does it necessarily signal that the food is no longer safe to eat.

According to guidelines set out by the German Food Bank, the average best-before date for some products is far too conservative.　We should remember that foods such as rice and pasta are often edible for a year after the date on the package.　Even products such as hard cheese are consumable for an extra 21 days, though a lot of care is usually needed.　Surprisingly, honey can also last as long as rice and pasta. It is still safe to eat yogurt for five days after the best-before date, and it is the same for ham.　You can safely eat bread for a few days after the best-before date but that time is shorter than for yogurt.　It is important for consumers to understand best-before dates correctly in order to reduce food waste at home.

Meanwhile, some other solutions to food waste problems have been developed. For example, some grocery stores in Canada are using a smartphone app to notify customers when food nearing its best-before date goes on sale.　This system targets shoppers who are interested in buying surplus products at low prices.

Also, the idea of "food sharing" is spreading globally. There are services that supply surplus foods at restaurants and supermarkets to those in need through charity organizations. This kind of service contributes to reducing food waste and decreasing poverty at the same time. Governments are also considering solutions for food waste problems. In France, supermarkets are legally required to donate surplus foods to charities or use them as animal feed.

Food is an indispensable part of human life. In order that everyone in the world can eat safe food sustainably, we should make choices in our lives that can reduce food waste.

35

(492 words)

Questions （目標3分）

1. A huge amount of food waste [1].

　① emits greenhouse gases, especially in developing countries

　② is based on correct understanding of best-before dates

　③ is caused by misunderstanding of best-before dates in developing countries

　④ results partly from inaccurate understanding of best-before dates

2. Of the following four graphs, which illustrates the "real" safe-to-eat time of each food the best?   [2]

①

Time after best-before dates that the following foods are still considered edible

Bread	+5 days
Ham	+2 days
Hard cheese	+3 weeks ... +1 year
Honey	
Rice, pasta	
Yogurt	+2 days ... +1 year

②

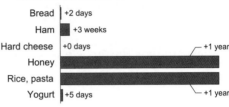

Time after best-before dates that the following foods are still considered edible

Bread	+2 days
Ham	+3 weeks
Hard cheese	+0 days ... +1 year
Honey	
Rice, pasta	
Yogurt	+5 days ... +1 year

③

Time after best-before dates that the following foods are still considered edible

Pasta	+2 days
Ham	+3 weeks
Hard cheese	+3 weeks ... +1 year
Honey	
Rice,bread	
Yogurt	+5 days ... +1 year

④

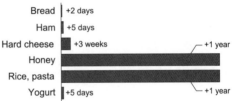

Time after best-before dates that the following foods are still considered edible

Bread	+2 days
Ham	+5 days
Hard cheese	+3 weeks ... +1 year
Honey	
Rice, pasta	
Yogurt	+5 days ... +1 year

3. According to the article, which two of the following statements correctly tell us the current situation of food waste problems?   (Choose two options.   The order does not matter.)   [3] · [4]

① A large amount of food is thrown away in an edible condition.

② Best-before dates of food are becoming longer and longer these days.

③ Best-before dates on a package of food indicate its safety.

④ More and more people are suffering from starvation because of the huge amount of food waste.

⑤ Various efforts have been made to solve food waste problems.

4. A smartphone app being used in Canada enables people to ⬚ 5 ⬚.
  ① know which foods are about to expire and buy them at discounted prices
  ② save time and effort when people go shopping at the local mall
  ③ see which local grocery stores sell food at the lowest prices
  ④ understand how inaccurate best-before dates are

5. The best title for this article is " ⬚ 6 ⬚."
  ① How to Deal with Food Waste Problems
  ② Making Guidelines for Setting Best-Before Dates
  ③ The Relationship between Food Waste and Poverty
  ④ Various Ways to Make Old Food Edible

スピーキング・トレーナー
◯³)) 本文を音読しよう ☐   492語÷ ⬚ 秒×60= ⬚ wpm